INTRODUCTION

Though offices are not a contemporaneous invention, there are few spaces whose identity is so closely linked to the 20th century's image as them.

If the factory is the essential backdrop to the 19th century then it is the place where the changes that sum it up took place: workers' movements were born there, the class concept and the dialectic which gave birth to the idea that mankind held of himself in that era; it is in a similar vein that the office evokes more than any other place our century's identity.

Offices in the last hundred years have occupied the hearts of cities, their most emblematic areas and have changed their physiognomy through their most characteristic architectonic expression, the skyscraper: a new, radical building that has become commonplace worldwide, changing the landscape, taking it over and projecting its own metaphors right before our very eyes.

Offices have also fostered one of the phenomena which has transfigured our society. We are now having to irrevocably face up to a new outlook of the world and relationships between men: the radical transformation of the communications systems.

These have grown and been developed in offices ever since its conceptual birth, giving rise to each and every one of the technical innovations in communications systems: the telephone, calculators, the fax, the computer,

..... each new stage in communications development has been received with enthusiasm in the office field. Not only furnishings have had to continually adapt to the new devices, rather that the new instruments have now become central to the office itself in an extremely short time frame indeed. Communications have changed offices and will continue to do so even more. Just like a virus entering a cell, it feeds off its own resources and ends up destroying itself, many of the elements configuring the essence of offices have been eliminated in a similar fashion: typewriters, accounting ledgers, endless files, ... have been replaced by more perfect systems more akin to the working logic of offices but which, at the same time, allow a glimpse of the disappearance of their classical conception and traditional ways.

Spaces for offices have taken two unquestionable concepts right to extreme limits in current society: rationality and efficiency. These have engendered their own brand of architecture and a paradigmatic aesthetic.

Perhaps for this very reason the office reflects, like no other place, some of the less welcoming features that have touched modern day mankind. Films such as Billy Wilder's *The apartment* or Jacques Tati's *Playtime* ironically unleash a parody on the underlying logic behind these kind of places and which draws our attention to the lack of identity or the sensation of being uprooted.

However, it is no less certain that in the last few years these same criticisms and caricatures have been used to highlight the latent lacks and the defects in this kind of space, they have become an object of reflection, in acquired experience and have allowed doors to be opened up towards other forms of conceiving offices, of making them more human, less standardised and closer to people themselves.

That is why it is not difficult, in the great majority of the furniture pieces presented in this book, to see that the designers have

responded to motivating forces different from those oftentimes associated with this kind of furnishing.

This is a logical, necessary evolution which must bring about variation in this kind of space, from primary, immediate, often ridiculous and dehumanised layouts, to more complex configurations and individualised wherever possible as regards the singular and emotive content.

That is why we believe that there is distance and experience enough for us to approach the subject of offices in the critical sense, in a less puerile, more conscious manner.

This book gathers together and evaluates the latest office furnishings models on offer. Examples completely different one from the other, very often appealing to opposing ideas.

We think that there is no better way of studying, knowing and comparing completely opposed ways of understanding the same type of furnishings, spaces and needs so as to attain ones own criteria thereby allowing the models to be chosen and spaces configured in an entirely personal way.

ACHILLE CASTIGLIONI

The Italian designer, Achille Castiglioni, has been and continues to be a constant reference point and model for all generations of designers ever since the forties. We have also wished to take him as a reference point and hence our dedicating this collection's first article to his latest incursions into the office furnishing arena. The Sangirolano office programme, the Vela dividing panels, the Quark desk, the Eta shelves and filing cabinets or the lights have one trait in common, a different way of comprehending what an office is, greatly distanced from the stereotyped image. Achille Castiglioni does not limit himself to providing a strictly functional answer to the needs associated with a specific type of furnishing, but instead accompanies his pieces with an emotive or ironical charge which allows them to not only suggest other ideas and sensations, but also to more easily establish a certain degree of complicity with the user.

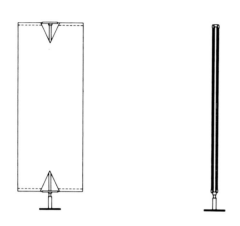

As the Italian designer and architect, Alessandro Mendini says: "Achille Castiglioni is a *theatrical* designer, because he introduces a spectacular character into his works, in addition to the functional and formal character. His objects are scenic instruments, leisurely functional, and suggest the possibility of a dynamic relationship to those enjoying them. They do not lend themselves to use layered with cold functionality, but instead stimulate a humorous identification, they are objects for action." (Introduction to the show catalogue *A la Castiglioni*, Barcelona 1995).

This is basically the concept, shift the emphasis from the object to the user. A natural and necessary operation which humanises the design because it requires thinking and the assuming of other factors cohichare different from the purely mechanical, ergonomic or spatial ones. Factors linked to the perception of things, to their intellectual and emotional interpretation. The user is first and foremost a person, not a morphological, abstract worker moving predictably. To feel comfortable, not only must their back not ache, but they must also feel a certain empathy towards the space and the elements surrounding them. ▪

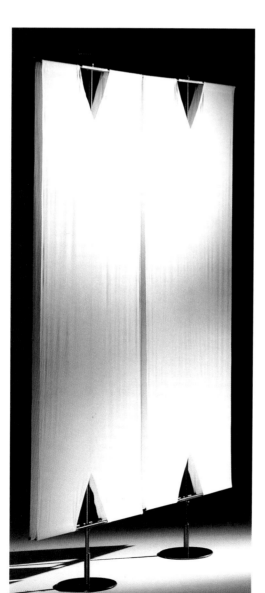

▶ *Composition of two Vela model dividing screens. This system allows as many sections to be coupled together as desired with whatever layout wished, due to the fact that no joints are present which predetermine the form.*

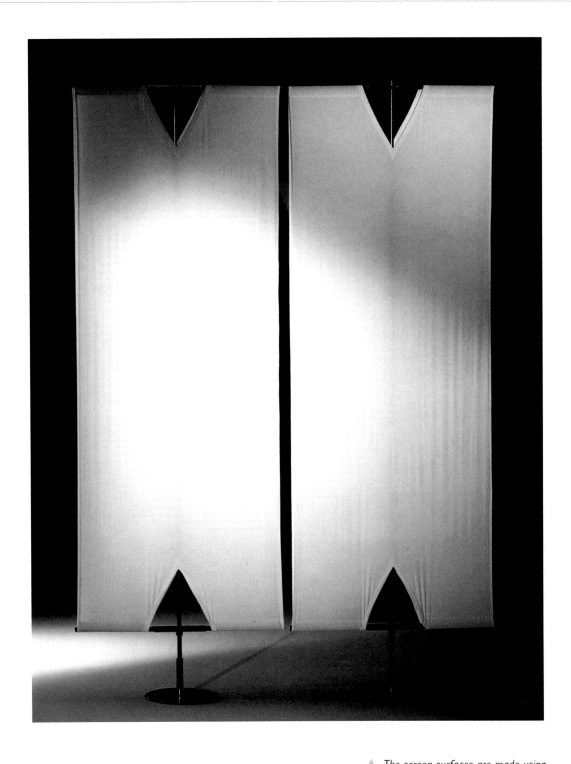

▲ The screen surfaces are made using white canvas which sets off the enormously suggestive interplay between shadows and transparencies. The material can be removed and is easily washable. The framework is comprised of black-lacquered tubes and the base is a circular plate made in the same material. Size 90 x 253 cm.

▲ The Eta bookcase is made using a solid
beechwood structure with movable shelves, with
or without doors. Finishes can be in either cherry,
walnut or in various coloured lacquers.

◀ To the left, the Quark desk, measuring
58 x 72 x 72 cm, a white-lacquered solid wood
structure which can incorporate shelves,
containers and side drawers made in the
same material.

▲ The Taraxacum hanging light is formed by 20 polished aluminium triangular faces and fitted with three 40W bulbs in each of them.

▲ Stylos standard lamp, 200 cm high - 17 cm diameter. It is comprised of a metal circular base and a white opaline polymethacrylate diffusor, fitted with a 150W bulb.

▲ *Brera diffuse lighting hanging light.*
The diffusor is made in white acid-
etched glass. The cables are rather
special, made from silicone and are
pull resistant.

▶ *The Brera lights also come in*
other versions: applique, soffit and
standard lamp

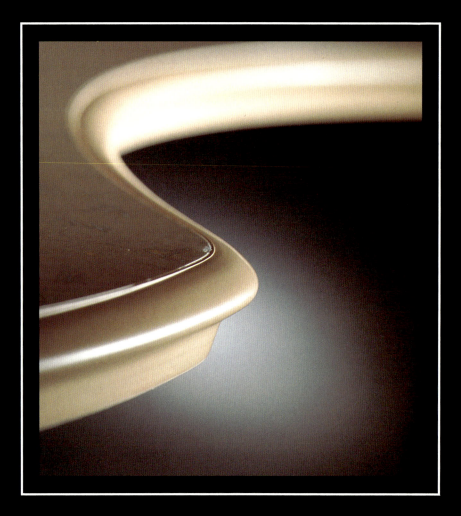

"Only in change is there continuity". The team of the Japanese designer based in Milan, Isao Hosoe, has designed a system to equip offices which is endowed with gentle lines and organic forms based on mobility and constant evolution.

The user can at anytime freely adapt the space to suit needs. Each activity has been considered on an independent basis, thereby ensuring that each function is autonomous and can be carried out separately. There is a specific connection system so that each element can be integrated into the work station, whatever the existing configuration be. Beyond the traditional separation between personal and common space, TNT stimulates the appearance of a shared space, preferentially assigned to a group or an activity

rather than to one individual alone. This place
can have a parallel life to that of the group
activity and detach itself from it when finished
with, once again integrating each element into
the individual work space.

The aesthetic adopted by the designers
deals with transmitting the dynamism and
fluidity that the spaces can attain. In this sense,
the product's final form is not only capable of
undergoing successive changes, but also
manages to transmit that same spirit via the

◄ *The forms of the different elements vary according to where they are placed within the global design of the office. There are transition, angular or wave-shaped typologies. The combination of some with others allows a sinuous, organic profile to be constructed. The peripheral elements can be very easily incorporated depending on what the activity to be carried out is at any given moment.*

▼ *Below, wiring detail. Both the DeltaFloor flooring and the different work station elements are prepared for installing all kinds of cables.*

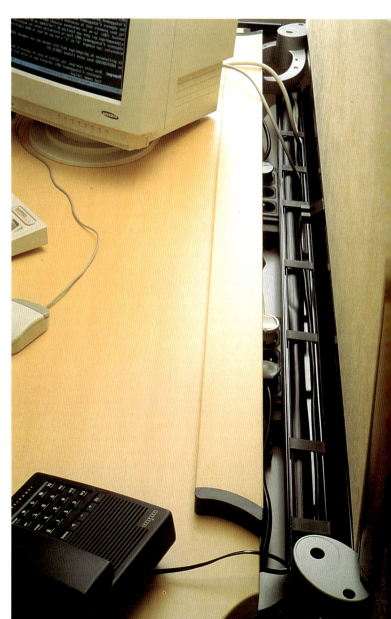

fluid profiles of the desks and the organic silhouettes of the legs.

In order to develop this concept, several families of elements have been created with different characteristics which, joined by extremely simple, quickly made connections, guarantee the permanent, ongoing adaptability of not only the work spaces, but also the company itself.

Thus, aside from the **nucleus** elements which define the main functions for each work station, the work tops and the legs, fixed or mobile, there are other additional series of elements grouped into three families: peripherals, nomadic and surroundings.
The tops are of different sorts and shapes i flat planes, transition, right-angled and wave-shaped planes. The combination of them constructs a sinuous organic profile which allows 90-degree turns to be accomplished. The work desks include their own stabilisers which hold the tops and legs by means of a connecting clip.

The **peripheral** elements provide the secondary functions and allow the evolution from a simple desk to a specific working space. The different types of shelves, tall classification cupboards, dividing screens, frontal panels and electrification channels are found in this family grouping.

The **nomadic** elements momentarily complete a configuration for group activity. They allow the space to be shared and stimulate interactions.

> ▶ *The nomadic elements stand out due to their great versatility. Isao Hosoe has endeavoured to make these elements capable of constantly evolving, thereby making short periods of group activity easier and their subsequent move to use in another activity.*

◀ *The furnishings designed by Isao Hosoe reflect an innovative concept of the relationships between colleagues in the same office. The TNT system's dynamic character is intimately associated with teamwork and fluid, permanent dialogue.*

The **surroundings** elements guarantee integration of the TNT system in the building. This family grouping includes both the DeltaFloor technical flooring and the specific lighting systems which provide the existing installations with flexibility and ongoing developmetal capacity.

The TNT system's key factor, that which makes it an effective, dynamic, variable system, is the kind of connections that have been designed by Isao Hosoe's team. The union of different elements takes place via a fixing clip which allows easy assembly in a few seconds of both tops, legs and the entire range of peripheral elements.

The nomadic and surroundings elements are structurally independent and are thus autonomously adaptable to the equipment fitted. The very profile of the nomadic desks allows them to be adapted to each other without the need for fixing them. ▪

Office desk and four quarter lamp

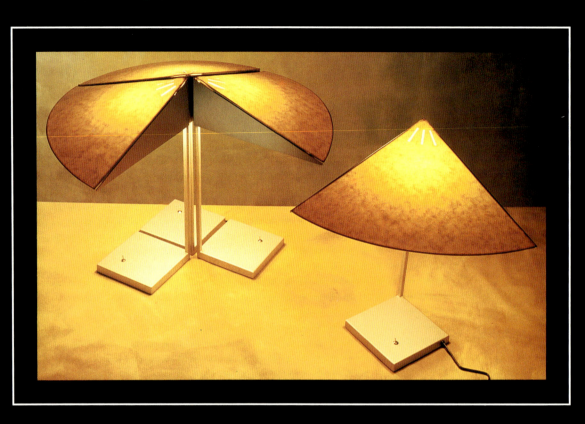

The office desk designed by Pedro Miralles displays an asymmetrical form which combines the straight volumes of the drawers with the curved planes of the top and rear section. The appearance is of a compact piece of furniture. It is made using ash wood stained greyish-green or pear-coloured sycamore. It rests on a highly polished or likewise polished nickel-plated steel base. Between the top and the drawers some metal structural pieces separating the different elements can be seen. The bureau has a practical central leather-bound border. ∎

▲ The four quarter lamp is the result of dividing the circumference of a shade into four quarters in such a way that each one of them is independent, and the final form can be either that of one quarter or successive additions until the full circumference is attained. The shade is Nomex. height 47 cm. E-14, 40-60W, 220V bulb.

▶ Two desk models with different finishes. Top, with drawers and filing system. Bottom, with single drawer.

DALE FAHNSTROM /
MICHAEL McCOY

Bulldog Chair Series

The series includes several models with different kinds of backs varying in height, the base, swivelling with five spokes with castors or runners (for visitors), and with or without armrests. However, all the models do bear the same ergonomic profile. They are made with a metal structure covered with polyurethane foam and upholstered in optionally-coloured cloth. The armrests and the rear of the seat back are leather upholstered. ▪

▲ *Onto the stool base with pneumatic height adjustment and five-spoked swivelling base with castors, has been added a Task type back to make this working chair rather taller than is normal, highly suitable for working at counters, drawing desks.... or other high tops.*

▶ *Professional chair with high back made, together with the seat, in a one-piece unit. The armrests in this typology are fitted to the seat back.*

▼ *The seat back on this model is a piece independent of the seat. Somewhat lower, meaning that the head cannot be rested on it as is the case of the previous model. Owing to it having an independent seat back, the armrests are fitted solely to the seat itself.*

▶ *This model, the executive chair, combines some of the elements found in the previous two: high, yet independent seat back and armrests fitted to the seat.*

31

◀ The visitor's chair has a runner base given that its role is completely different to that of working chairs. In this case, movement must not be permitted, though comfort should be maintained. Nevertheless, it must be remembered that this is a chair for waiting a short while only.

◀ The different models are usually associated with different working stations depending on the height of the seat back, or whether it has armrests or not. This model is designed for young executives or managers.

▶ A view of the two different seat backs. Both are made in polyurethane, cloth upholstered and with the rear of the seat back upholstered in synthetic leather.

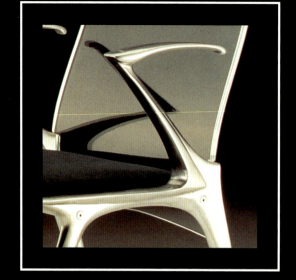

The Meteora chair is designed as a series of pieces which can be taken apart. The structure, comprised of two elements formed by the legs and the armrests, is made in polished aluminium. The back is fitted into the structure as an independent piece. It comes in both varnished wood and methacrylate. Its almost rectangular, though somewhat curved, shape, adapts to the form of the user. The seat is padded with polyurethane foam and upholstered with Alcántara cloth which comes in different colours and tones.

Each one of the pieces, though conceived as an independent removable part, is designed with the express purpose of giving the chair's final appearance a unitary look. Nevertheless, certain details reveal this model's specific singularity. The armrests, for example, do not have any element joining them to the back, but are instead supported by an oblique bar which forms an acute angle on the front vertex and is fitted into the topmost part of the rear legs.

The unitary piece formed by the legs and the armrests is highly suggestive given that the designer has made torsion thicker those sections where the structure must bear greater stresses of flexing or torsion, hence the chair manages to formally convey the distribution of the forces arising.

Both by the materials used and by the chair's very form, the general appearance combines a certain coldness with a sophisticated simplicity. Thus, it is highly suited for conferring a certain ambience to

specific office spaces, such as waiting or
meeting rooms, where the user of chairs is not
continuous, but also where it is desirable to
convey a certain character. ■

▲ *The Meteora chair combines several
independent removable pieces. In this case, the
back is made of methacrylate, but also comes in
varnished wood. In spite of the different materials
used in the pieces, the chair manages to convey a
unitary appearance.*

35

Summit and Staff

Summit System is an office desk and cupboard programme designed by the technical department of the Coopsette company, the intention being to offer maximum versatility. The basic structure of the system consists of a U-shaped carrying beam to which different feet and tops are fitted. Height is adjustable which means that the work tops can be at different levels in accord with the activity to be carried out. The beam is prepared for chaining together in broken lines and specific tops have been designed which allow corners to be worked thereby achieving the desired layout. The desks are fitted with conduits for telephones, lighting and computer connections and come in either melamine or wood. There are an enormous amount of accessories such as drawers or trays which can be fitted. ▪

◀ Fully equipped open angle desk., with shelves
for the printer paper and the computer keyboard.
The tops are melamine and have bevelled rounded
edges. The matching cupboards form part of the
Summit programme.

▲ Office desk with varnished
and polished wooden top. The feet are
black-painted metal. This example shows
the Summit programme's simplest
configuration.

The Staff system, just like the previous programme, is conceived to meet all the needs of those office spaces by offering a global furnishing programme. The different possibilities allow both individual and linear or multiple work spaces with tables for meetings.

It is Coopsette's philosophy to offer an economical, simple, complete and functional system.

The desk's structural system is also a single horizontal continuous beam which allows the wiring required to be channelled through it. The supports in this case are dark grey coloured oblique bars in the sharpe of a trestle. The tops can come in wood, glass or melamine in various different colours and tones. The system incorporates cast fixing joints. The cupboards, bookcases and drawers are made using the same materials and finishes with the aim of achieving a unified appearance. ▪

An example of the *Staff System* with a C-shaped linear layout, with two examples of filing cabinets of different height.

The basic concept behind the *Staff* and *Summit* systems is the same: a central beam which makes the required layouts possible, and which allows the necessary telephone, electrical or computer cables to be incorporated.

39

BALDANZI & NOVELLI

Formula and New Pony

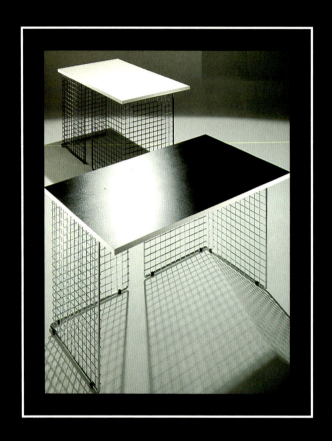

The Formula desk stands out because of its top being held by an electro-welded metal grid, chromed or epoxy varnished in a variety of optional colours. The grid merges with its own shadow thrown onto the floor. It expands so that its limits become indistinguishable.

This grid also admits numerous hanging accessories made in the same material, such as trays or baskets. The designers have configured a setting of associated elements: filing systems, drawers or grills for hanging on the walls.

The New Pony model responds to a more common idea. It is comprised of a structure of two chromed or varnished steel trestles which each incorporate latticework trays on the lower sections. The top can be either black melamine or tempered glass. ▪

▲ The Formula desk comes in two varieties according to whether the grid is L-shaped, covering the rear of the desk, or circumscribing the side planes only. The tops come in either white or black melamine.

41

▲ A view of the New Pony desk surrounded by other elements such as the rear bookcase, chair, desk lamp or pencil holder with similar finishes. Baldanzi & Novelli manage to associate the conceptual desthetics of their pieces with a pragmatic, functional design.

▶ The reducing of the finishes of the tops to the most elemental colours or to a simple transparent glass surface, doubtlessly comes from the designers' desire to make their pieces using the minimum amount of resources.

GABRIEL TEIXIDÓ

Nikkei, Track, Lavoro, Montera

▲ A view of the Nikkei manager's desk and the
Lavoro chair. The designer has combined two colours
in both cases: black and red.

▶ On the following page, overall view of the
desk with another of the same chair models.
The desk top is rosewood veneered DM and the
sides are covered with semi-leather.

The Nikkei manager's desk and the Track office programme have one characteristic in common which makes them similar, despite, at first glance, their appearing to be completely different. Both models are formed by clearly defined planes, separated one from the other by metal pieces which stop the elements enclosing the side of the desks forming a with the top. This means that each element meets up with a different part and facilitates the combining of different materials and colours.

The top on the Nikkei desk is made using DM veneered with lignum vitae, on a highly rigid metal structure. The legs and drawers are made in wood, but are covered with black semi-leather. A metal folder covered with the same material can be optionally fitted onto the desk top.

The Track office programme stands out by its apparent lightness. In comparison to the Nikkei desk where red and black are combined here, the designer has opted for less dramatic, softer colours: a green and a greyish-blue, the matt metallic grey of the pieces of this material and the light-coloured wood of the tops.

Track is also designed for shared work spaces. The desks can be joined together to form corners, the separating screens do ensure a certain degree of privacy. ▪

◀ *The Track programme includes different-sized cupboards and filing systems finished in the same materials and colours as the desks. The separating screens are 1,130 cm high. The metal structure allows cables to be fitted inside.*

▲ *The tops come in either beech or pear wood, or beige melamine. The sides are available in blue, green or beige. On the following pages, an illustration of a desk with a top which combines the writing space with that for meetings.*

47

▲ The Montera chair is designed so that the different elements can be added or taken out thereby attaining a chair fitting to individual needs. On this model, the part of the back jutting out from the armrests is covered in black leather in contrast to the rest of the chair, upholstered in red cloth.

On this version of the Montera chair, a back with a straighter profile than the one in the top illustration has been used.

Two different-sized versions from the Lavoro seating programme. This model form is slightly zoomorphic. By the shape of the armrests, the chair appears to embrace its occupant.

51

TOSHIYUKI KITA

Atlantis

▲ The appearance of the chairs varies according to the
kind of structure chosen in the main. On this page, the
two models belonging to the middle type, while overleaf,
the detail of the model assigned to management posts
can be fully appreciated.

The Atlantis series designed by Toshiyuki Kita contains three different models which can also come in three different finishes. Though the seat body and back are the same on the three models, the carrying structure and armrests do vary. While all the models are made using steel covered with polyurethane, the simplest model is not fitted with the optional articulation for adjusting the seat back and the legs are fixed. The steel structure can be either chromed or plasticized. The seat and back are made using either leather- or cloth-upholstered polyurethane.

What makes this chair's appearance singular, is the back above all else. On the lower section it is narrower than the top, a gentle curve on the back gives it a heart-shaped appearance. ■

JESÚS GUIBELALDE

Univer

The system designed by Jesús Guibelalde is comprised of four different elements which can be combined with each other to configure a work desk of varying complexity.

The carrying structure is formed by a system of vertical panels and horizontal metal bars of varying heights in such a way that the tops overlap one and ther at different levels.

The system allows drawers to be incorporated which hang off the structure's bars

The general appearance of the Univer system is made up of pure geometric forms of different textures and colours which are superimposed among themselves.

Materials of highly varying characteristics have been used. The tops can come in either wood or tempered or embossed glass. The drawers can take the ruddy hue of walnut or be made using rosewood. The colour and hue of the lacquering of the metal structure can also be varied.

▲ *Illustration of a configuration comprising the
four elements of the Univer system. In this case, the
desk is U-shaped with right angles, on one of the ends
a circular meeting table has been incorporated.*

◄ *On the previous page, top, detail of the overlaps of the different modules of different height. The different levels mark out a hierarchy of spaces with the aim of each one of them appertaining to a different activity.*

▼ *On the left, a simple configuration comprised of two elements only. In this case, the tops are both in transparent glass thereby leaving the structure of the desk in plain view. Rosewood has been used to make the drawers.*

◄ *Below, L-shaped layout. The circular desk extends the working area and facilitates possible meetings. The drawers are made in walnut. The metal structure is light-grey lacquered. The contrast of colours and different geometrical shapes is one of the traits defining the look of the Univer programme.*

RUD THYGESEN / JOHNNY SØRENSEN

Royal

Rud Thygesen and Johnny Sorensen have taken great pains to introduce a series of furnishings characterised by extreme simplicity into the office setting.

All the elements have been designed with a high pureness of forms. Wood is the material used almost exclusively. Solid oak, beech, mahogany or maple, finished with a double coat of hardened varnish.

The Royal series' appearance is not commonly found in a furniture family grouping where complex layouts, full of accessories and devices, very often abound.

The Royal desk is comprised solely of a top and four legs, one at each corner. Two small drawers on the front section are introduced inside the top leaving only the handles visible.

The office desk designed by Thygesen and Sorensen supposes a different conceptualisation of the workplace. Here, the forms suggest a less mechanised ambience. ▪

▶ *Almost empty desks. Cables lacking. Renouncing complexity in the workplace implies a different attitude.*

JAUME TRESSERRA

Targett, Paralelas, Nobel, Prólogo and Samuro

Jaume Tresserra has managed to confer a personal image of singular coherency to all of his work. His furniture does not appear to belong to any epoch, yet ahways immediately identifies with valuable objects which require preserving and care.

The simplicity of all his pieces, the forceful geometric forms incorporate incredibly subtle details which manage to transfigure the global look. Behind the apparent simplicity lies a universe of singular elements on another scale revealing countless semi-hidden possibilities: every gesture, detail and need has been studied and resolved. The apparent contention of the forms arises from the respect held for the materials and a deep faith in their inherent elegance.

He always works with highly noble materials, mainly walnut wood finished with natural varnishes applied by hand, with specific brass pieces treated in electrolytic baths to obtain high quality finishes: sulphurised, chromed or plated. ■

◀ A view of the Targett desk writing area, made using oak root wood. The inkwells and the small compartments used for holding accoutrements are found incorporated into the desk top.

▲ General view of the Targett manager's desk. The materials used on the furniture designed by Tresserra are always the highest quality. The wood is hand-varnished walnut. The desk measures 74 x 85 x 210 cm.

61

◀ A view of the Targett desk Buck. The measurements of each drawer is studied according to the objects they have to hold.

▶ General view of the Paralelas desk. Its general measurements are 74 x 80 x 190 cm.

▼ A view of the Paralelas manager's desk. The metal fittings have been made using chrome finishes. The apparent simplicity of the global appearance is combined with the taste for detail.

In recent years, Jaume Tresserra has designed three executive desk models called: Targett, Paralelas and the most recent one, Nobel. All the models are made using walnut wood finished with natural varnishes. On the central space of the desk, Tresserra introduces pieces made of different materials, such as oak root wood or Vaquetilla leather which define the surrounding space where work is carried out preferentially. Around this central space, other elements have been incorporated such as inkwells or plummier, which barely rise above the desk top.

Next to the desk, Tresserra has designed the corresponding bucks using the same material and an identical philosophy. No knobs or handles, the exterior appearance does without the sensationalist elements in favour or some materials of maximum quality and exquisite finishes. The different-sized drawers are studied for storage and filing both folders and typological instruments of differing sizes. ◾

◀ On the sides of the desk, a foldaway top holding a perkary leather plummier. The leatherwork uses the same material.

▲ On the following pages, a general view of the Nobel desk. The central part corresponds to a Vaquetilla leather plummier/book rest.

63

◀ *The bucks are on a pivot. The left buck (top) has an extendible buck and three plummiers. The right buck (below) presents an extendible wing and a filing drawer. The interiors are natural burnished wood.*

▼ *A view of the Vaquetilla leather book rest.*

Jaume Tresserra mistrusts ambiguity. In most of his furniture pieces, needs have been clearly studied and interpreted. He endeavours to make his models comply exactly with the function they have been designed for and does not think it proper to add parallel accessories or additional elements which detract from the main role of the piece.

All of this is paradigmatic on the Prologue bookcase. Tresserra has exclusively conceived a holder for books and all their accoutrements: numberers, alphabetic signals, trays or book rests, ... are at the service of books and their classification.

The materials used are his customary ones: walnut wood, stainless steel fittings and accessories and Vaquetilla leather. ■

◄ *This page, different views of the Prologue bookcase. General view, detail of the mounting foot adjuster, of the numeric or alphabetical signallers for classification and the mountings with lighting accessories.*

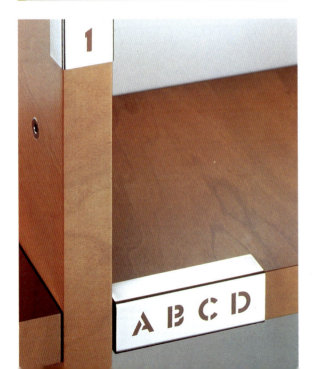

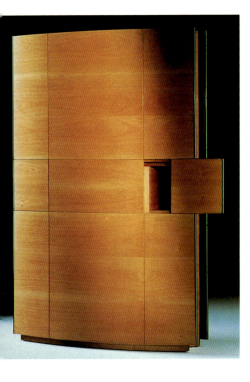

Samuro is one of the most characteristic pieces of furniture from the Jaume Tresserra collection. Its clean forms, ascetic appearance, combined with the care taken over every last detail, reveal the fascination this Catalan designer feels for traditional Oriental culture and aesthetics.

Samuro is without a shadow of doubt a silent furniture piece, yet all the while hinting at keeping innumerable images and secrets. In fact, on its exquisite white varnished walnut surface, the traces of many widely varied-size compartments can be read, almost seeming to be made to hold exactly the object placed in them.

Perhaps Samuro expresses with greater clarity than any other of Tresserra's pieces of furniture the designer's desire to foment the private, intimate relationship between the object and its owner. Samuro appears to be destined for keeping small treasures replete with images. ■

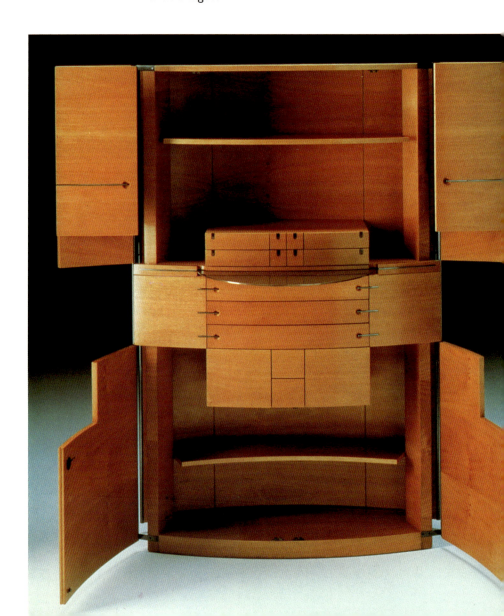

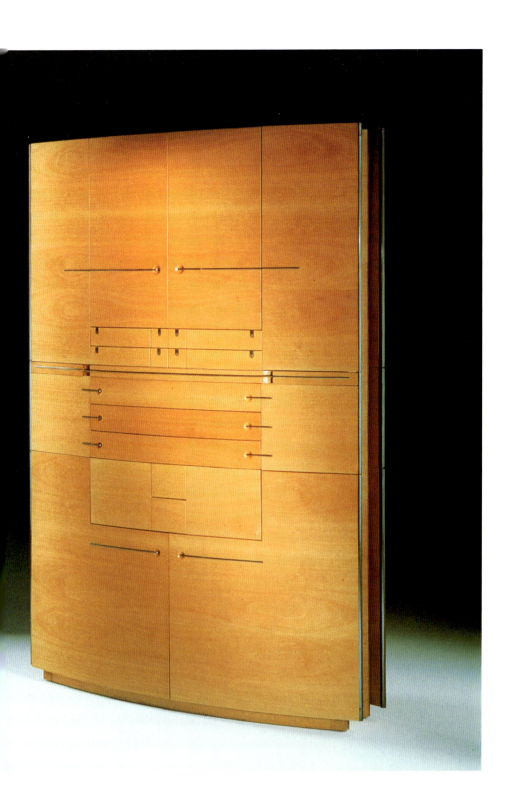

▲ The appearance of the Samuro furniture piece depends entirely on whether it is open or closed. In the centre, a swivelling half moon-shaped tray is shown.

▲ The overall appearance of the furniture piece conveys a certain hermeticism. It seems to be made for solely keeping secret objects of singular value. The wood used is varnished white walnut. The handles are sulphurised brass.

LUCA MEDA

Misura, Progetto 25 and PL Screens

The series of office furniture designed by Luca Meda allows very simple elements to be combined. All of them are made in extruded aluminium, in light, mainly white, tones. This type of finish gives a better reflection of light.

Progetto 25 is a system of extruded metal screens to which doors and windows can be added. These screens allow large open spaces to be divided up into compartments. Depending on the height of the screens, the isolation of the spaces can be either total or solely up to the height of the person seated. The screens are prepared for receiving desks and hanging shelves. The modules bear a markedly horizontal character, which makes them differ substantially from the PL screens which are sub-divided vertically.

The surface of the PL screens is perforated laminate filled with sound proofing materials. The panels can be covered with pure wool cloth. The outer profile is formed by an extruded aluminium rail which allows accessories to be hung off it. There is also a version made in double-paned glass whose purpose is to further improve acoustic insulation.

▲ *Top, a view of the elements comprising the Misura series. This series combines rectangular tops with inverted T-shaped feet, cubic drawers and backing panels hung from the edge of the desk of a width similar to the work tops. The result is a clearly visual, conceptual system.*

▲ *A view of the Progetto 25 screens. The desks are fitted into the screens themselves. Just above the top, a narrow longitudinal window communicates both sides.*

▲ *Top, an example of an office layout where the
PL screens and Misura furnishings have been
combined. The different heights of the screen modules
sketch a broken profile. The cubic forms of the
shelves hung on the screens are reminiscent of the
volumes of a city's buildings.*

◀ *A varied set of office containers made
in stamped extruded aluminium. A lip on
the upper edge of the drawer allows
handles to be done away with.*

PETER HIORT-LORENSEN and JOHANNES FOERSOM

Campus Chair

The Campus model came from the idea of creating a light, easily stackable and transportable chair, which would at the same time be elegant and comfortable. The Campus chair does not belong to the typology of the classical office chair, but instead constitutes an ideal complement for those activities which do not take place continually. Hence the frequent use of this chair in working meetings and conferences.

▲ The Campus model, by its very simpleness and light weight, is ideal for occasional use in equipping spaces for conferences and meetings.

▶ The curved forms of the seat and the wooden back and the simplicity of the metal structure, characterise a model combining elegance with functionality.

The moulding of the seat and back accentuate its lightness and give it a characteristic appearance.

The Campus chair weighs a mere 4.1 Kg. The chairs can be stacked with or without the armrests. In rows of several chairs, the silhouette of the curved back forms a highly suggestive image which manages to convey the idea of unity.

The optional armrest comes in two kinds of finishes: in beechwood or polyurethane. The Campus model can be complemented with a writing support, plus a set of links for linear rows and a stacking trolley. The wood can be varnished in an extensive range of colours and hues, or upholstered in different materials. The metal structure can be either chromed or lacquered. ■

▲ *Above, a view of a group of chairs placed in rows. The curved backs give a dynamic, suggestive image to the rows.*

◀ *On the previous page, a view of the basic model. Beechwood or polyurethane armrests can be fitted to the Campus chair, as well as a writing support.*

▶ *The designers have studied with great care the stacking and storing of the chairs, this can be done very easily indeed with both the simple model and the one fitted with armrests.*

T he Swift chair range is a family grouping of different models with distinct finishes and colours, all of them designed by Antoni Riera in collaboration with the AF Steelcase Strafor design department, with the shared desire of achieving a flexible chair that can be used for different activities and is adaptable to the different characteristics of people.

What particularly stands out to a great degree in this family group of chairs is their capacity to regulate the positions relative to the different components. In addition to adjusting the seat and armrest height, differing forms of coordinating the relative movements of the seat and back can be opted for: the tilting of both can be synchronised or, the possibility exists of keeping the seat fixed while the back tilts, and of course, the option to lock the multi positional mechanism is also included. Adjustment is done via a lever found underneath the seat itself.

The end purpose of each model can be adapted to not only the different preferences of one person alone for carrying out different activities at any given time, but also to the demands of work stations, meeting rooms and offices shared by different areas and individuals in the same office. ▩

▲ *The models vary according to the user's preferences. With the Swift seating range, it is not only possible to personalise the finishes and the upholstery colours, but to also incorporate or leave out the armrests, castors or spoked feet, depending*

The model designed by Fabio Lombardo constitutes a sophisticated variation of such a simple typology as a top supported by trestles. The materials chosen, aluminium in the main, as well as the finishes of the pieces and the resolution of the details, give it a technological appearance, similar to that of a precision instrument or machine.

Far from being a rhetorical image, this model's form expresses the latent complexity behind an apparently simple typology, thereby evincing the technical effort required in making it in a precise manner.

Both the legs and the prop bar are made in epoxy-enamelled extruded aluminium which comes in dark green, Cypriot pink or natural sheen. The brackets supporting the top are fixed to the prop bar and are made in sanded pressure-cast aluminium and transparently enamelled. The tops can be either rectangular or rounded and are made in light and dark grey-toned postformed plastic. They can also come veneered in birch, beech, pear or even in glass. Height and inclination are adjustable, the bars being prepared for its electrification. Fittable accessories in various finishes have also been designed.

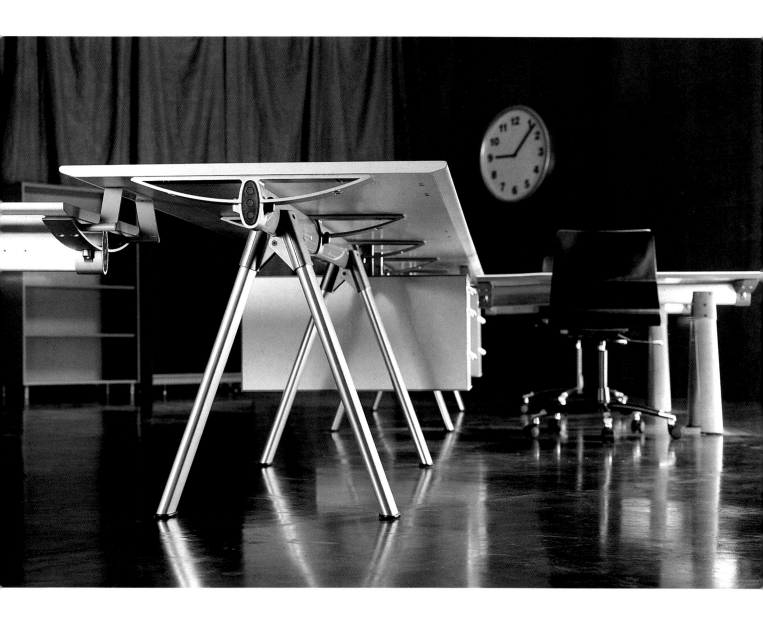

◀ *A view of the articulation and the bracket supporting the tops. The finishes and materials convey an image associated to technology and precision. The supports are prepared for the fitting of cables and communications lines.*

▲ *View of the carrying structure and the lower mechanism in an adaptation for desks linked together. The overall aspect is of great solidness. The desks' tops can be supplied in other kinds of materials such as wood or glass.*

81

▲ ▶ Two versions of the AeTo/P lamp, in applique and standard lamp, completely directable. The diffusor is coloured metallised glass and the structure aluminum. Fitted with 300W halogen lamps.

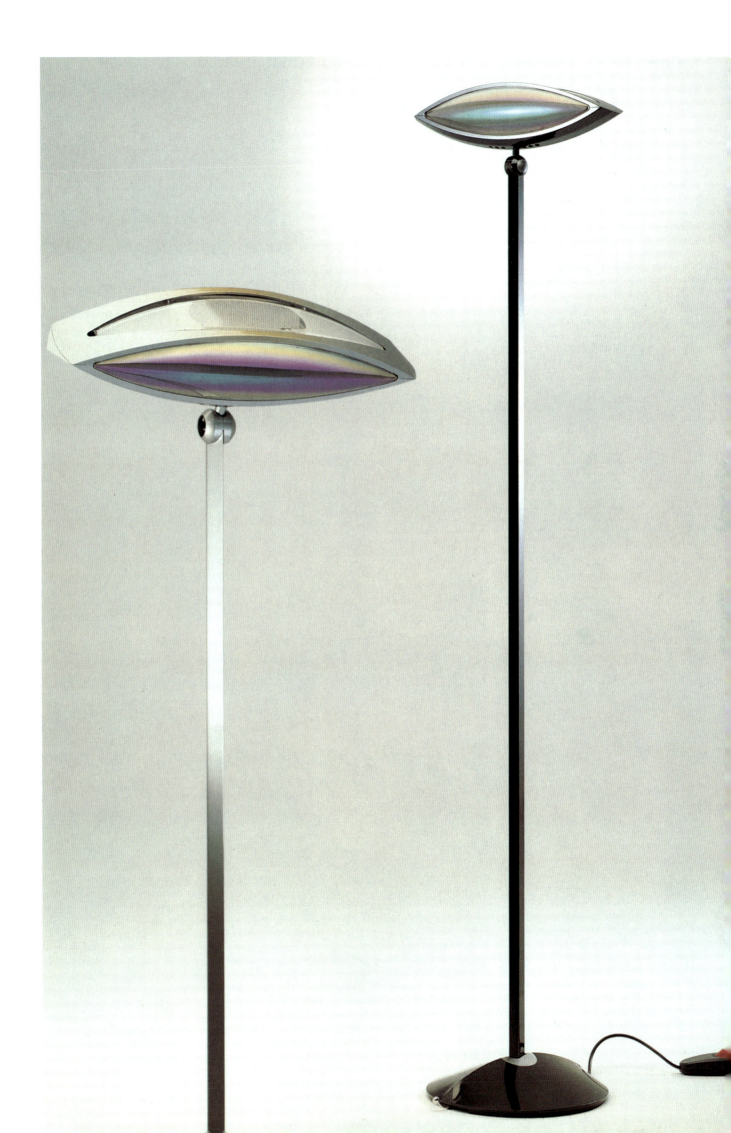

OCTAVIO MESTRE

Spider

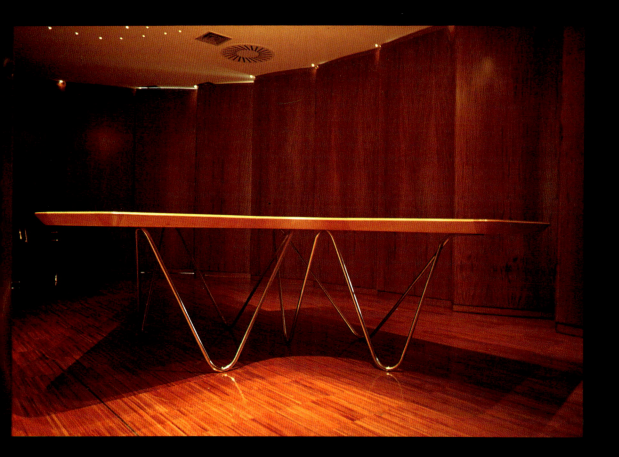

The meeting table designed by Octavio Mestre changes the relationship between participants. The irregular outline, inspired by organic forms, introduces an inevitable dynamism. A slight asymmetry can help to convey a greater fluidity in the setting. Far from being an impediment, this may provoke relations to settle, freeing up the initial static state. In this way, Octavio Mestre has taken up the concept of functionality into more subtle arenas. ■

► *The structure of the table is made using curved metal tubing tracing a sinuous perimetral line, converting it into a metaphor for the very same fluidity it wants to provoke.*

LLUÍS PAU

232-CV and ÀBAC

The 232-cv bookcase and the Àbac furniture piece are completely different in appearance, however, the two pieces coincide in their ability to be adapted for holding very dissimilar objects: files, books, accessories, stationery material,... The office furniture is normally designed for exact functions, these ambivalent elements turn out to be incredibly useful because they can be adapted with much greater ease. Both pieces introduce singular forms into the office environment which qualify and lend character to the space. ▨

▲ ▷   *The structure of the 232-cv bookcase is comprised of 232 horizontal and 52 vertical metal rods. It comes with or without castors. Assembly is simplicity itself and, as can be seen from the numerous examples shown, it offers a great variety of possibilities.*

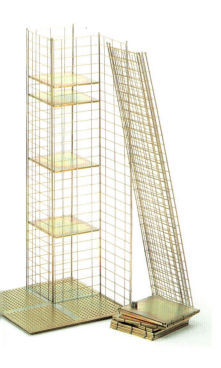

87

▲ ▶   *Lluis Pau designed the Àbac furniture piece in collaboration with the architects Martorell, Bohigas and Mackay. The piece consists of a tower subdivided up into multiple containers of varying sizes and different functions on each one of its faces. The central structure can be made in black lacquered wood or varnished sycamore, while the peripheral containers are lacquered in either black, red or blue.*

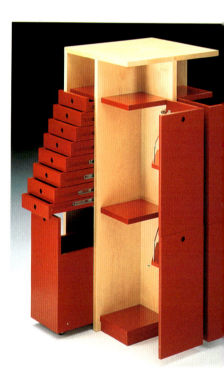

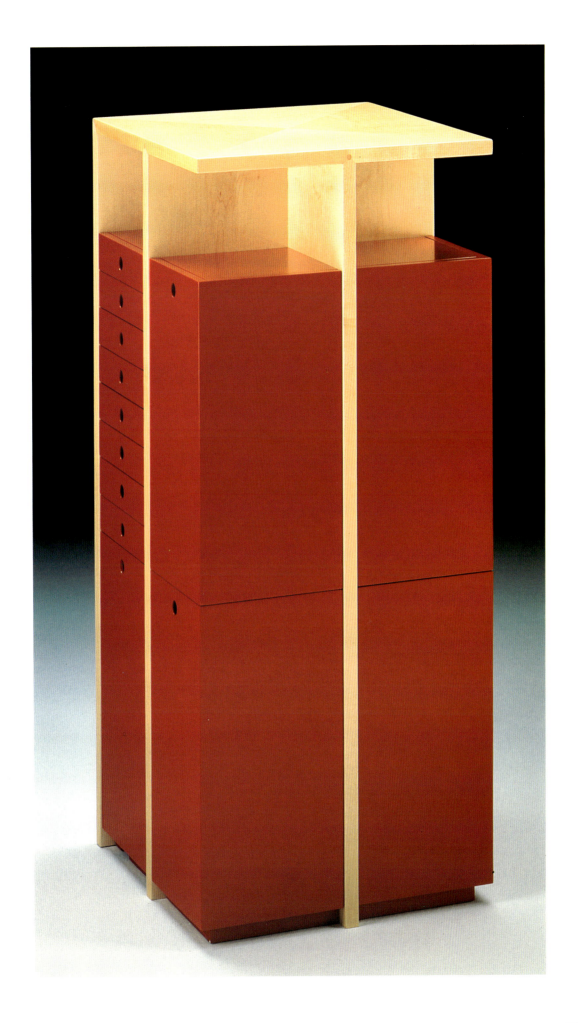

BURKHARD VOGTHERR

Spin

"**P**rogress is also defined as elimination":
with this phrase, the German designer,
Burkhard Vogtherr sums up the philosophy
which has led him to design the Spin chair. This
model, while drawing together all the
technological innovations as regards flexibility
and ergonomics, also gives a different
appearance, sober while still being elegant at
the same time.

Without doubt, what clearly makes this
model radically different from the rest of the
office chairs is its stylised, very long back.
Vogtherr has, up to a point, managed to
introduce into the office setting the
extraordinarily distinctive spirit of some of the
chairs designed by the Scottish architect, C. R.
Mackintosh dating from the turn of the century.
Nevertheless, the approach here is different,
given that as opposed to the rigidity of
Mackintosh's models, the Spin model
incorporates those mechanisms required to
adapt it to continuous use.

The name Spin is derived from the word spindle, one of the distinctive characteristics of this chair. A screw-threaded shaft which when turned raises or lowers the chair one centimetre per turn. Once the height has been thus adjusted, the mechanism disconnects when the chair is sat on. This system is guaranteed for up to five years.

The seat back can reach up to back or head height, and is endowed with the flexibility required to adapt to the user's movements. The form of the seat back follows the curves appropriate to the back in any position.

The front third of the seat is inclined downwards at a 14° angle thereby avoiding undue pressure on the arteries in the thighs, muscular tension in the legs and excessive weight loading on the feet when the user's body is leaning forwards.

The remaining two thirds of the seat stays in the horizontal plane thus ensuring comfort, while maintaining the body's centre of gravity and balance stable and avoiding sliding around.

The user can choose between four different armrest models, innovative amongst which and worthy of mention, is a movable armrest called "Mickey Mouse's ears". ▧

◄ *The singular measurements of the elements of the Spin chair, such as the seat back or armrests, configure this model's characteristic form. This particular appearance has not meant leaving out the latest innovations in flexibility and ergonomics.*

On page 91, the chair's appearance varies considerably when the seat back is lower and the armrests are of a different typology.

UMBERTO RIVA

UR 303

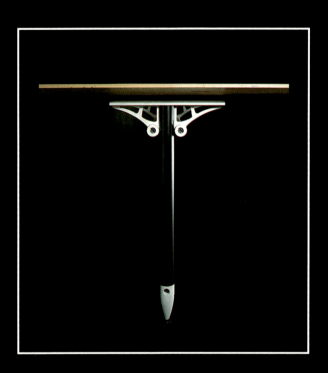

Umberto Riva has managed to combine great overall simplicity with certain surprising, sophisticated details which transfigure the manager's desk from the appearance of the UR 303 office programme and make it less immediate.

These details are found on the upper and lower ends of the desklegs of a desk four legs. The four steel tube legs rest on pointed aluminium pieces which manage to convey the sensation of a desk resting on the floor. At the same time, the upper part of the legs are joined to the structure holding the top by some singularly shaped, double volute aluminium pieces that, apart from adjusting the upper plane, also introduce an appearance halfway between an exact technological solution and a parody of it.

The UR 303 programme allows the desk to be completed with variable-sized wheeled drawers and containers.

◀ *On the previous page, a view of one of the desk legs. The aluminium pieces introduce a surprising, ironical nuance which mixes technology with sensuality.*

▲ *Umberto Riva has used materials of greatly diverging characteristics in order to achieve a suggestive appearance with a highly evocative appeal. The top is made in Finnish birch, the legs are steel and the connecting pieces aluminium.*

LOGIC OFFICE FURNITURE

Logic Furniture System

The design department of the British company, Logic Office Furniture, Ltd. has created a complete furnishing and dividing screen system for office layouts.

Each one of the elements is prepared to form part of a whole setting or be used independently.

The structure of the components is made using steel, with tops, frontals and panels in melamine, wood or laminates.

▲ *An example of the one of the programmes for the reception area. It is very interesting indeed to study the relationship established between the reception counter and the next office through the screens.*

The contrast of colours and materials is one of
the resources used by this British firm's designers for
conveying a greater vitality to the setting.
The programme's different components can be placed
both independently or forming layouts as shown
in this illustration here.

The Logic Office Furniture designers have paid special attention to the study of the visual relationships between the different working areas. In this sense, the dividing screens create interesting semi-transparencies between the different spaces via incredibly fine woven screens.

The British firm's designers have also accentuated the contrast between colours and materials: garnet and black, wood and moquette, ... with the intention of conveying a greater vitality to the work setting. ■

▲ An example of an operative area with a star or cruciform layout. The medium height dividing panels ensure the independence of each workplace while favouring communication between colleagues.

▼ *The dividing panels are made using double glass with the aim of improving the acoustic insulation of the offices. The luminosity of the wood contrasts with the darkened glass unfurling an attractive interplay between light and dark contrasts.*

LES BUZAN

Erance system

The Erance system, designed by Les Buzan for the British Vickers Furniture Company, offers a modular system for offices which includes a wide range of elements that can be used either independently, or integrated in settings with a homogenous, coherent image. The system tries to make compatible the functionality and versatility inherent to this kind of furnishing, with more relaxed aesthetics which are able to convey a certain cheerfulness to the work place. In this vein, Les Buzan has opted to use a wide range of colours and to soften the outlines of some accessories such as filing cabinets, trays or pencil holders.

The system also incorporates steel-framed dividing panels coming with different optional finishes, as well as several models of ergonomically designed chairs. ■

◄ *On the previous page, secretary's and reception desk finished in a soft grey hue. The lilac colour of the chair and other accessories combines*
perfectly with the general soft grey conveying an image of serenity.

▲ *A view of one of the office configurations with work tops finished in wood. The dividing panels allow the tables to be rested against them and shelves and filing systems to be hung from them.*

101

MARIO RUIZ

Global and Net

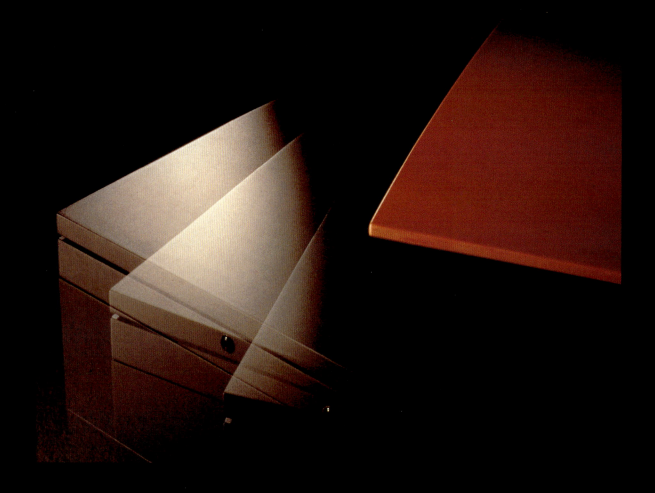

The idea for the Global programme came from the manufacturing company Bordonabe's plans to incorporate in its new catalogue an office furnishing programme, which would diversify from the company's customary product line, furnishings of high class and quality for top level management, to extend it into other market segments.

Mario Ruiz himself commented on the design: "In order to optimise the product while maintaining quality, the path lies in the rationalisation of the entire proposed series. An extensive programme has been achieved in

the Global programme using very few pieces
indeed, which greatly simplifies many aspects.
The strategy has been to have all the parts and
elements properly available, avoiding as much
as possible the use of complements and
accessories that were not absolutely essential.
The legs, for example, have been replaced by
containers when these appear."

Following this approach, and with the aim of
maximally holding down the product's final
price while logically still maintaining both quality
and rigour, resources have been optimised,
both in production terms and in those
concerning the configuration of the series itself.

▲ General view of one of the variations.
Despite being comprised of three elements
only, the Global system allows up to
sixty-six variations.

103

In producing the Global series, the Bordonabe company's production system was optimised thereby allowing production of gently curving profiled surfaces to be totally automated, which in this case is translated into five different forms.

In this way, the office adapts to the person and not vice versa. Wood, pear or rosewood, stands out on the desk tops and among the elements comprising the series.

Starting with basically three elements, the three versions of the product are achieved, some of them are shown in the illustrations accompanying the text.

With this programme it is possible to achieve up to sixty-six different variations of the combination of tops, metal legs (where neither buck nor leaf are used), frontal skirtings, bucks and leaves. The latter two constitute, in the majority of the versions, the legs for the work tops, without any other elements added on. The buck, with central locking and electrical wiring system, turns around on itself, thereby optimising adaptation to each user. This element also allows the presence of inordinate amounts of cables draped over the furniture to be avoided, given that they are fitted inside it. As office complements, Global includes joint desks and cupboards with vertical shelves. ▪

▲ A view of one of the configurations of the Net programme. The work top curves meet both ergonomic demands and aesthetic aspects.

▶ The work tops can be made in both wood and stratified coverings. The panels and folding separating screens, finished in texturised lacquer, can include the individual company's corporate colour scheme.

The Net programme offers, at reasonable cost, different solutions for operative posts. Its offerings cover practically all of the conventional configurations of office installations, and additionally provides, thanks to a purified modular concept, a creative, fresh and motivating interpretation of the work space.

The Net system incorporates three support types, in extruded aluminium, steel or textured wood. The tops, in natural wood or stratified covering, are made with different curve groupings which meet ergonomic and aesthetic demands.

Both the working surfaces and legs contain solutions for wiring electrical and electronic components up. The filling and drawer modules are made using components which guarantee perfect working throughout the lifetime of the furniture. There is a wide range of finishes available in different coloured, textured lacquers.

An imaginative range of accessories -folding screens, panels, skirtings- provide freshness and colour to the units, offering the added possibility of personalising and harmonising the furnishings with the individual company's corporate colour scheme. ■

GEMMA BERNAL
RAMON ISERN

Facto

In the Factor seating programme, Gemma Bernal and Ramon Isern have adapted one type of chassis to different models of chairs while varying the feet. Thus, though the Facto programme includes chairs, visiting chairs and even waiting room benches, the appearance of the family grouping has a sole character which is highly suited to homogenising the seating in large office spaces. The chassis has successfully solved the problem of the lumbar area, one of the regions of the back where most pain is produced as a result of working long hours in static positions.

The base can come in both spokes with castors and a continuous tubular structure from the armrests to the feet. The seat back can reach up to shoulder height or be extended above head height. There is a smaller-sized model, the Mini Facto, of great interest for domestic spaces. ■

▲ On this page, a view of the Facto
programme Syncron model; continuous
tubular structure from feet to armrests. The
designers have solved lumbar problems in a
particularly efficient manner.

▶ The Facto Bench is an extension of
the office chair programme which
follows the same design ideas and
choice of materials.
The bench assembly and coupling has
been particularly well thought out.

ESTEL

Kronos

The Kronos programme presented by the Italian company Estel, allows different elements to be combined around a basic layout comprised of a manager's desk and an annexe table for holding meetings.

A series of auxiliary shelves allow all the accessories and technical support

▲ *On this page, a view of the Coros chair designed by Fabio Gigli for the Estel company. It is highly appropriate for conveying a comfortable ambience to visitors.*

▲ ▶ *On this page, several views of the Kronos system. One single layout, L-shaped in the case shown here, it can be formed using different components and comes in varying finishes: glass, black lacquer or grey anthracite.*

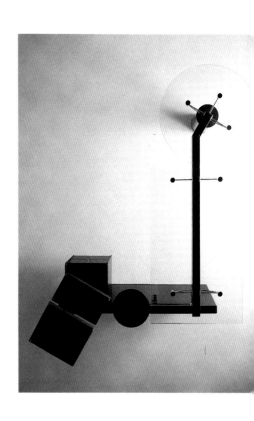

115

◀ *The 4x4 screen system allows the incorporation of peripheral desks set into the walls and different-sized filing cupboards.*

necessary to be fitted: computer screen, telephone, fax, ...

The general form of the Kronos system conveys a dynamic, versatile and efficient image.

The finishes vary from the warmth of wood to those surfaces conveying a more technological image, such as glass or black lacquer.

The Estel company has completed this furnishing series with the design of a spatial distribution wall system for offices, the 4x4 system. Various kinds of walls or screens have been created: dividing, aggregated, equipped or WS, with an extensive range of coverings which allow offices to be personalised: woods, gloss lacquers, fabrics in numerous colours. ▪

An example of an office equipped with the 4x4 screen system. In this case, different models made with distinct materials have been combined. The manager's desk is the Kronos model and the chair situated next to the auxiliary meeting table is the Coros.

The Italian company Ebrille's design department has developed three complete programmes for offices incorporating all kinds of furnishings. The Skyros and Skorpios programmes are aimed at directors' offices, while the Myconos series contains simpler models.

Although the materials and finishes are different, all of them offer a wide range of elements which include the working desks, accessories, telephone holders and meeting tables, in the case of the programmes for directors, or reception and public service counters in the Myconos series.

◄ *On the previous page, a director's desk from the Skyros programme. This system offers a range of elements made in walnut or ash veneered chipboard, rounded edges with no burrs.*

▲ *This page, director's desk combined with an auxiliary meeting table. The various finishes, polyurethane resin varnish, walnut or black stained allow different chromatic combinations.*

121

◀ *On the previous page, examples from the Skorpios furnishing range. This is designed to offer a homogenous image based on the elegance of the wood. All the elements are made in varnished Italian walnut veneer. The cupboard doors can be in either this material or dark glass.*

▲ *Administration setting furnished from the Myconos programme. The furniture is made using a chipboard structure covered with stratified plastic. The finishes come in ivory, light grey or walnut colours.*

123

AFRA AND TOBIA SCARPA

ATS, Filo, Pierrot and Papillona

▲ On this page, one of the versions of the ATS
dividing wall systems. The modules can be
equipped with hanging containers, organised
both horizontally and vertically. The carrying
structure is made of steel with levelling feet.
The covering can be either melamine, extruded
aluminium varnished with dark green epoxy
resin or glass.

The Filo chair is made using a chromed tubing structure with a runner base. It also comes with a swivelling, five-spoked base with castors. The seat and back are made in ash wood.

It is specifically designed for easy stacking. Hence, aligned with its light weight, it is highly suitable for conferences or occasional meetings. With this aim in mind, Afra and Tobia Scarpa have designed some pieces which allow them to be laterally joined up at the base, this being particularly useful when forming rows. ■

▲ *As can be seen in the top illustration, the Filo chair can incorporate small variations such as adding or removing the armrests or changing the runner base for a swivelling spoked one, thereby making it open to the greatest number of adaptations possible.*

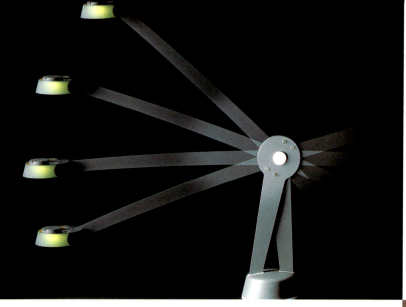

▶ The Pierrot desk lamp comes in two versions in which the type of light used varies, this can be either direct or indirect and diffused. The base and head are made in coloured techno-polymers, while the articulated arm and the vertical support are made using composite materials.

▲ The Pierrot lamp's central ball-and-socket joint allows it to assume different positions making it highly appropriate as a reading lamp. It is fitted with a toroidal transformer located in its base. The halogen lamp is 12V-50W. The maximum attainable height and length are 98 cm and 88 cm respectively. The base diameter measures 15 cm.

Afra and Tobia Scarpa have been designing lights for thirty years. Their models not only incorporate the latest technological advances, but have also been significant innovations in their own right. Two of their latest models, highly suitable for offices, are the Pierrot desk lamp and the Papillona standard lamp. ■

▶ The Papillona standard lamp provides both direct and indirect diffused light via the two prismatic diffusor-reflector glasses. It is 192 cm high.

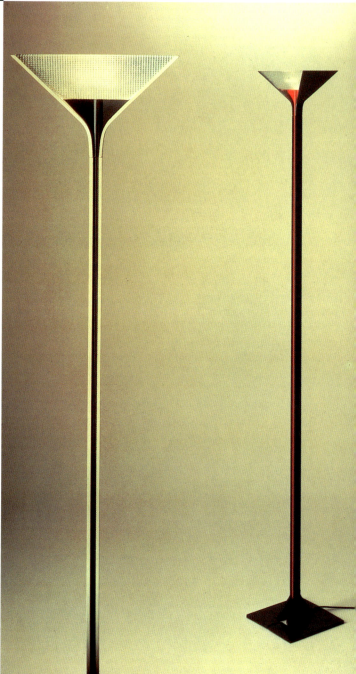

LIGHTS
AND
ACCESSORIES

PHILIPPE STARCK

Eve, Romeo Moon, Oa, Ara and Dr. No

▲ OA desk lamp. The glass and flower are handmade. It is fitted with a touch dimmer device allowing the flower to be placed in any position desired.

▶ On the following page, the directable Arà desk lamp shaped like a horn and made in chromed metal. It is fitted with a 35W-12V halogen lamp. Height -56.5 cm, diameter - 17.5 cm.

Objects designed by Philippe Starck are the fruit of a love story, the one this French designer enjoys with the world of objects. His seductive capacity could only come from the imaginative flow of a creator seduced and in love. His forms capture the sensuality and irony of this strange idyll between a man and things.

Starck has managed to bring back to industrial design the sensuality of some sculptors' works from the first half of the century, such as Arp or Brancusi, and the irony of more recent artistic movements like Pop or Postmodernism, conveying this to the objects surrounding us. ▪

▲ *Philippe Starck himself holds the Romeo Moon diffuse ceiling light in his mouth. The outer corona is pressed glass and the inside diffusor of satined glass. The upper diameter measures 30 cm, the lower 50 cm, the crown is 22.5 cm high and the maximum length of the three steel cables is 4 m.*

▶ *The Dr. No chair is made in polypropylene with extruded aluminium feet and finished in warm, luminous colours: yellows, greens, oranges, ... and can be easily stacked. It is designed more for resting than working, hence it is more suited for visiting or waiting rooms.*

▲ *Eve diffuse lighting standard lamp. Of
classical forms, the diffusor screen is
handmade in Murano glass,
height - 195 cm.*

Galileo

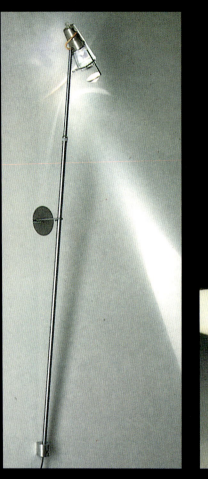

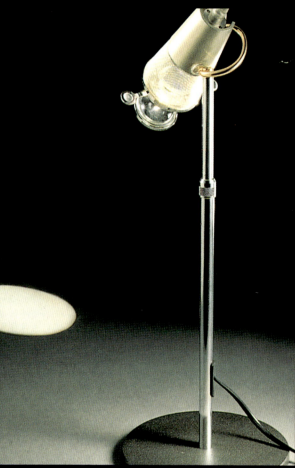

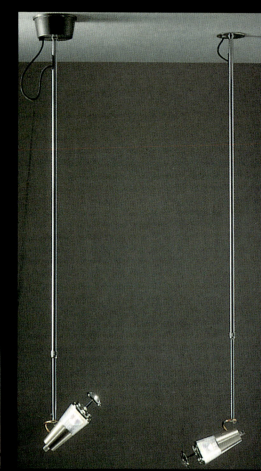

The Galileo system offers different variations of the same light. Though it comes in standard lamp, ceiling, desktop and wall models, the differences arise exclusively in the support itself, given that the actual lamp is the same. The 50W halogen reflector is dichroic, and is fitted with an adjustable diaphragm and lens on a movable aluminium support which allows the light beam to be varied.

The circular base is made of steel plate and the shaft is a telescopic steel tube allowing the height to be adjusted. ▪

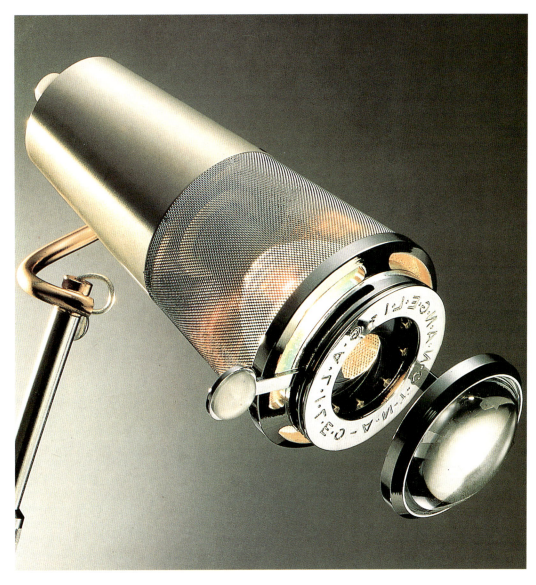

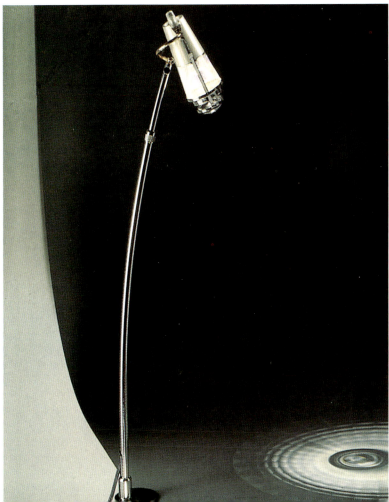

◀ ▲ The Galileo light bears certain similarities to a photographic camera, such as the diaphragm or lens. Its appearance is deliberately technological.

135

JUAN AUGE

Eclipse, Japan, Alien, Kairos and Grifo

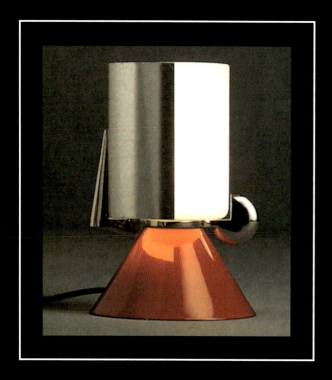

▲ On this page, the Eclipse model: desk top lamp with directable aluminium reflector, adjustable by means of a chromed cast piece. The base is metal, painted in red, green or grey. Height - 24 cm, base diameter - 15 cm. E-27, 60W bulb.

▷ On the following page, top left, two of the four versions from the Japan lamp collection (standard, ceiling, desktop and applique). The structure combines bibinga wood and chromed brass. Nomex shade. E-27 bulb of up to 150W rating.

▷ Alien applique, polished cast aluminium structure and curved diffusor of translucent glass or polished copper. Fitted with a 150W bayonet halogen lamp. Height: 55 cm. Diffusor: 20 cm

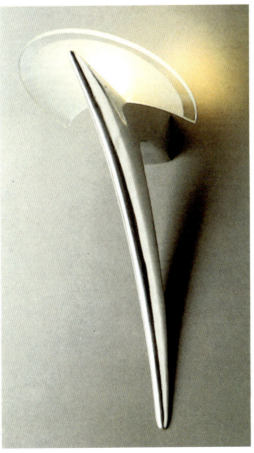

▲ Top, Kairos standard lamp. Also comes in applique version. The base is black-painted cast metal. The arm is a tubular bar of natural or black anodised aluminium. The shade in white or blue glass. It comes fitted with a brightness controller. Height: 197 cm. R-7S, 300W bulb.

▲ Grifo is a wall applique made in polished or white-painted cast aluminium. The diffusor is opalised glass for the E-14, 60W bulb. The shade measures 8 cm and is 22 cm long.

137

STEPHAN COPELAND

Tango

The features of the Tango lamp designed by Stephen Copeland allow it, merely by replacing one base for another, to change into a desktop or wall model. The desktop model can also have a circular base or fixing system for locating it on the edge of the desk. This versatility mainly comes from the two-tubed structure with flexible joints which allow it to adopt all positions required. The light source can also be articulated thanks to a ball-and-socket fixing. The diffusor is coloured and opalised, fitted with a 50W 12V bulb. ▪

▲ *The appearance of the Tango lamp seems to have been inspired by zoomorphic forms, on an animal's skeleton or on an insect's filiform body. Thanks to the structure of flexible joints, the lamp's movements take place in a continuous fashion, without aggression. The structural tubes can present slightly independent profiles which give a subtle sensation of movement.*

VICENTE SOTO

Shia and Vogue

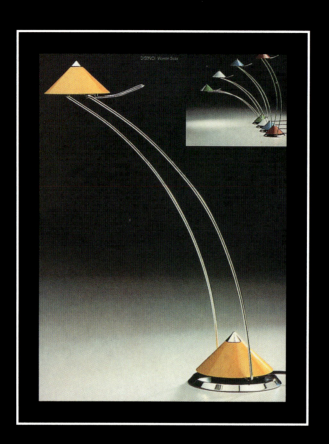

The head of the Shia lamp has a swivel range of almost 180°. thus making it a hand-sized kind of sun.

The head and the base are identical. Two metal conical pieces with the surface painted in one of the optional colours, all except the apex which has been left chromed. This therefore establishes an immediate relationship between the head and the base, a dialogue continued, which seems to be represented by the fine chromed steel curved bars which comprise the structure of the lamp.

*◀ ▲ The Shia lamp's different positions.
Of pure, geometrical forms, on work tops it
becomes almost a sculptural piece.*

141

▲ *Desktop model of the Vogue
lamp. It is made in a chromed steel
structure with an articulated arm in the
same material. The base, shade and a
small spherical counterweight on the
other end of the arm are made of
black metal. The maximum height
attained is 76 cm.*

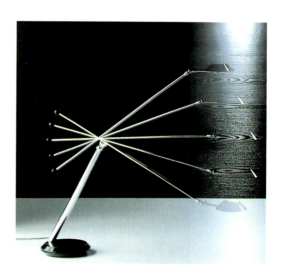

▶ *Composition with the different positions
the desktop lamp can adopt.*

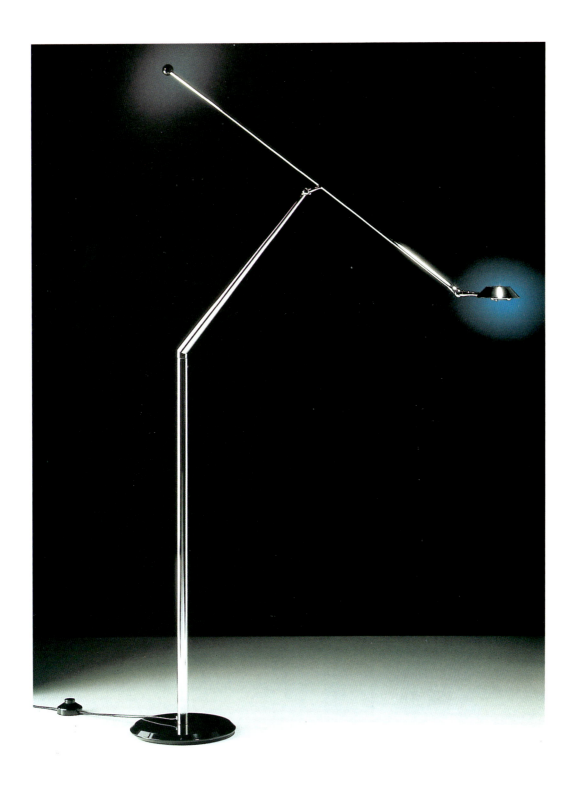

▲ The standard lamp is triply articulated:
midway along the main tube, the arm joint
and the head joint. The Vicente Soto design
searches for the greatest simplicity of forms
possible. The switch on this model
is base-mounted.

143

▲ *On the left of this page, a view of the Maru ceiling*

light, made in Japanese paper and hanging from

▶ *On the left of the following page, the*

Savoie ceiling light designed by Donato

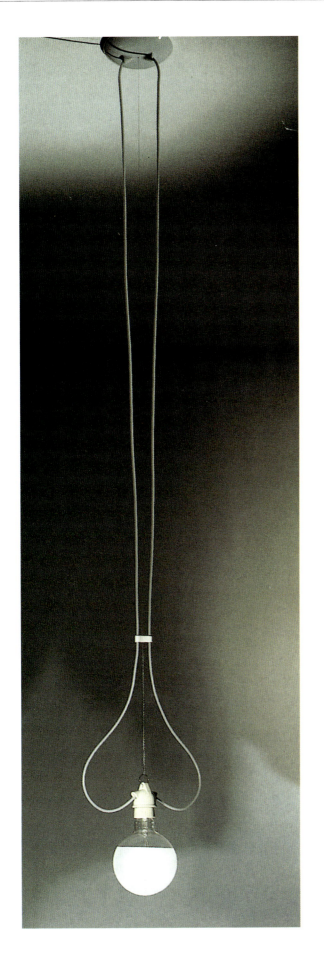

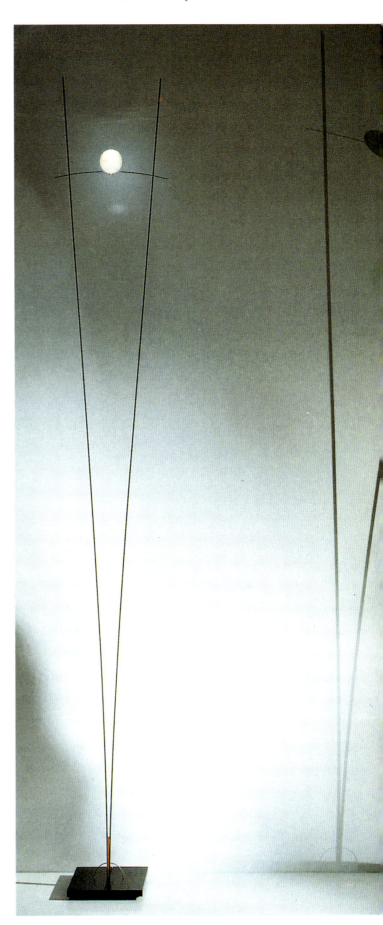

C. BERMUDO

Okele, Adil, Loa and Faro

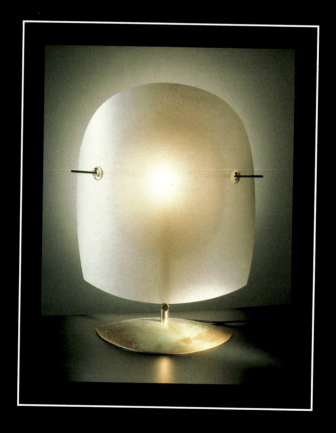

Lights designed by C. Bermudo always have singular, evocative forms. They are reminiscent of already used futuristic images or symbolic objects of an indecipherable nature.
Hence their capacity to introduce emotional images linked to the individual into oftentimes impersonal settings such as

▲ *On this page, a view of the Okele desk lamp. Made using polished or oxidised brass for the structure and base, parchment shade and incandescent bulb.*

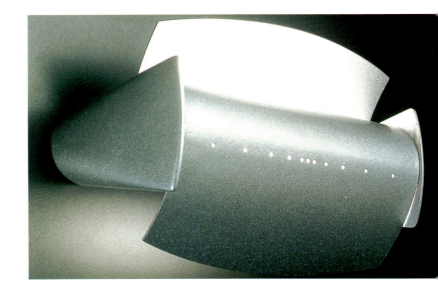

▶ *Adil wall lamp, fitted with an adjustable direction device for the light consisting of a series of highly versatile movable wings.*

▼ *Loa desk lamp. Both the base and the double-arm carrying structure are made in copper. The shade is toned glass and is covered by a mesh of chromed metal weave.*

▼ *The Faro desk lamp allows double illumination, toned setting and direct. It is designed primarily as a reading lamp. Made as a one-piece metal structure.*

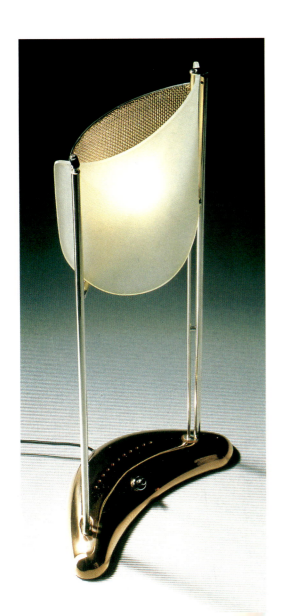

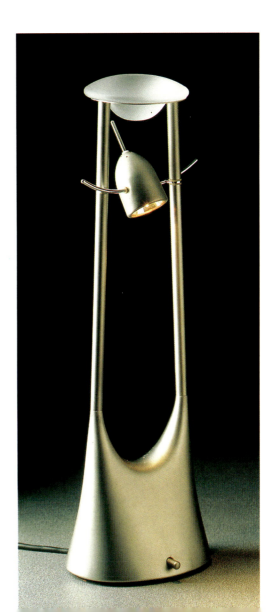

ROBERTO PAMIO

Land

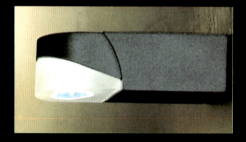

The Land series designed by Roberto Pamio comprises a family of standard and desk lamps and wall lights. The two former ones have a reclinable chromed metal double rod structure. The lampholder is a lacquered metal piece with a blue-toned Murano glass detail.

The sharpe of the applique is similar to the lampholder of the standard and desk lamps, though here the piece is articulated to enable adjustment of the light's direction. ▪

▲ *On the left, a view of the desk lamp's different positions.*

▲ *Two examples of the wall applique, one of the black lacquered and the other a light grey, almost white, hue. The applique can be oriented both towards the floor and the ceiling as the head is articulated.*

▶ *On the following page, a view of the standard lamp's different positions.*

P. A. KING AND S. MIRANDA

Aries

The ARIES programme for suspended, softlight or applique fluorescent lighting is especially designed for workplaces. Its large slats spread the light out enriching the quality of the main lighting source. All the versions are made in aluminium, powder painted, and with sanded glass slats. They come in both monotube and bitube versions. ■

▲ On this page, a view of the suspension lights with sanded glass slats. They have been designed to configure continuous lighting systems, all the while preserving the individual character of each one of the fluorescent tubes.

▶ On the following page, two wall applique models, vertical and horizontal. Both versions use compact, low power consumption light sources.

JORGE PENSI

Batela, Marie, Taps and Calenda

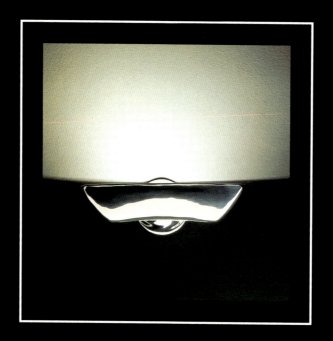

The Batela, Marie and Taps lights from the Argentinian designer, Jorge Pensi, are made using cast aluminium. All of them are fitted with halogen lamps.

Rounded shapes and simple components, supported on steel tubes, they evoke the lightness of birds, their brittle skeletons, their incomplete presence, always on the point of taking flight.

The polished, rounded surface of the aluminium is like that of a pebble trapped on the bed of a river, scattering reflections back up to the surface to attract the attention of a child to rescue it from its prison. ▪

▷ *Two Batela model lights. On this page the wall applique and on the following, the adjustable height standard lamp. Jorge Pensi has combined stainless steel with cast aluminium in the structure.*

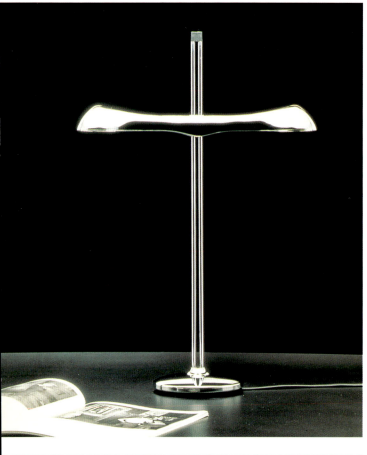

▲ Top, one of the wall
applique versions of the
Batela light.

▲ Top left, Marie desk lamp. This shows a
perfectly symmetrical shape, fitted with two
halogen lamps. It is especially designed for
reading and writing. The shade is height-
adjustable.

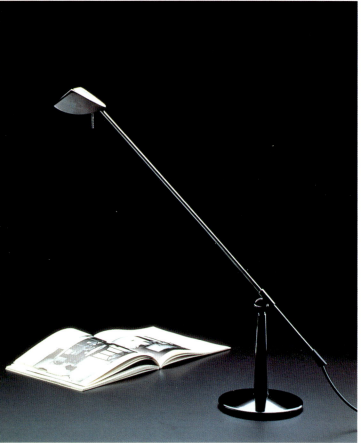

◄ Taps desk lamp, designed to be fully
articulated. Made in stainless steel or
black lacquer finish.

► Calenda series pencil holder. The
cylinder has the upper cut bevelled so that the
shorter elements can be placed in the lower
compartments and still remain in sight.

Jorge Pensi has, together with Carme Casares, designed a collection of accessories for offices: trays, pencil holders, ... All the objects are based on three extruded aluminium sections which are repeated on the different models, combined with plexiglass surfaces. The beauty of the unit develops forms of great simplicity. The designers have been guided in the main by strictly functional criteria, not only in the use of the accessories, but also when making them. Nevertheless, the purity of line and the frugality of the formal resources achieved is capable of transmitting a coherent aesthetic identity to the whole series. ■

▼ *Rollholder for Sellotape. The roll is suspended from the counterweight in such a way that the size of the rollholder is made notably smaller, it measures 14 x 8 x 5 cm.*

▶ *Two-compartment box for penholders
and writing implements,
made in aluminium, measuring
30 x 11, 3 x 7.2 cm.*

*◀ A view of the tray coupling system.
The extruded aluminium sections
comprising the basis of the Calenda
accessories system.*

157

► ACHILLE CASTIGLIONI
- Sangirolano:
  Olivetti Synthesis, SPA (Italy)
- Vela, Eta, Quark:
  BBB Over, SRL (Italy)
- Stylos, Taraxacum, Brera:
  Flos (Brescia, Italy)

► ISAO HOSOE
- TNT: Steelcase Strafor (Strasbourg, France)

► PEDRO MIRALLES
- Cuatro cuartos: Vapor (Spain)
- Mesa de dirección: Artespaña (Spain)

► DALE FAHNSTROM/MICHAEL McCOY
- Bulldog Chair Serie:
  Knoll Internacional (France)

► ANTONI RIERA
- Meteora:
  Chueca Hermanos, SL (Spain)

► COOPSETTE
- Summit, Staff: Coopsette (Italy)

► BALDANZI & NOVELLI
- Formula, New Pony: Frezza, SRL (Italya)

► GABRIEL TEIXIDÓ
- Nikkei, Lavoro, Montera:
  Axa Internacional (Spain)
- Track:
  Airidi (Girona, Spain)

► TOSHIYUKI KITA
- Atlantis: Casas (Spain)

► JESÚS GUIBELALDE
- Univer: Imat (Spain)

► RUD THYGESEN/ JOHNY SORENSEN
- Royal: Botium (Denmark)

► JAUME TRESSERRA
- Targett, Paralelas, Nobel, Prólogo, Samuro:
  J.Tresserra Design, SL (Barcelona, Spain)

► LUCA MEDA
- Misura, Progetto 25, PL: Unifor (Italy)

► PETER HIORT-LORESEN/JOHANNES FOERSOM
- Campus:
  Lammhults Möbel AB (Lammhults, Sweden)

► ANTONI FLORES
- Swift:
  Steelcase Strafor (Estrasburgo, France)

► FABIO LOMBARDO
- FL 201: IB Office (Italy)
- AeTo/P: Flos (Brescia, Italy)

► LLUIS PAU
- 232-CV, Àbac: Colur, SA (Spain)

► BURKHARD VOGTHERR
- Spin: Fritz Hansen (Allerrod, Denmark)

▶ UMBERTO RIVA
- UR 303: *IB Office (Italy)*

▶ LOGIC OFFICE FURNITURE
- Sistema Logic Furniture:
  Logic Office Furniture, LTD (Great Britain)

▶ LES BUZAN
- Sistema Evans:
  Vickers Furniture, LTD (Great Britain)

▶ MARIO RUIZ
- Global, Net: *Bordonabe (Vitoria, Spain)*

▶ GEMMA BERNAL/RAMON ISERN
- Facto: *Nova Norma, SA (Spain)*

▶ ESTEL
- Kronos, Koros, 4 x 4: *Estel, SPA (Italy)*

▶ EBRILLE
- Skyros, Skorpios y Myconos:
  Ebrille, SPA (Italy)

▶ AFRA Y TOBIA SCARPA
- ATS: *IB Office (Italy)*
- Filo: *Unifor (Italia)*
- Pierrot, Papillona: *Flos (Brescia, Italy)*

▶ PHILIPPE STARCK
- Eve, Romeo, Oa, Ara:
  Flos (Brescia, Italy)

▶ A. SILVA
- *Antonangeli, SRL (Italy)*

▶ JUAN AUGE
- Eclipse, Japan, Alien, Kairo, Grifo:
  DLC, SA (Spain)

▶ STEPHAN COPELAND
Tango: *Arteluce (Italy)*

▶ VICENTE SOTO
- Shia, Vogue:
  Manufacturas Celda, SA (Spain)

▶ INGO MAURER
- Maru, Flotation, Oh Jack!, Savoie, Ilios:
  Ingo Maurer GMBH (Spain)

▶ C.BERMUDO
- Okele, Adil, Loa, Faro:
  Marset Iluminación, SA (Spain)

▶ ROBERTO PAMIO
- Land: *Leucos (Italy)*

▶ P.A. KING/S.MIRANDA
- Aries: *Flos (Brescia, Italy)*

▶ JORGE PENSI
- Batela, Marie, Taps: *B. Lux (Spain)*
- Calenda: *Sabat Selección, SA (Spain)*